Eyelets for Scrapbooks

Sarah McKenna

SEARCH PRESS

First published in Great Britain 2005

Search Press Limited
Wellwood, North Farm Road,
Tunbridge Wells, Kent TN2 3DR

Text copyright © Sarah McKenna 2005

Photographs by Roddy Paine Photographic Studios
Photographs and design copyright © Search Press Ltd 2005

ISBN 1 84448 075 5   7451593

The Publishers and author can accept no responsibility for any consequences arising from the information, advice or instructions given in this publication.

Readers are permitted to reproduce any of the items/patterns in this book for their personal use, or for the purposes of selling for charity, free of charge and without the prior permission of the Publishers. Any use of the items/patterns for commercial purposes is not permitted without the prior permission of the Publishers.

Suppliers
If you have difficulty in obtaining any of the materials and equipment mentioned in this book, then please write to the Publishers, at the address above, for a current list of stockists, including firms who operate a mail-order service. This list also details some of the fonts used in scrapbooking projects.

Publisher's note
All the step-by-step photographs in this book feature the author, Sarah McKenna, demonstrating scrapbooking. No models have been used.

Manufactured by Classicscan Pte Ltd Singapore
Printed in Malaysia by Times Offset (M) Sdn Bhd

For my best friend, Victoria, who got me into all this in the first place!

Acknowledgements
I would like to thank:
Martin, Emma, Annie, Charlsie and Katie for many things, but especially showing great fortitude in the face of the camera lens!
Victoria for introducing me to scrapbooking, her unstinting support, extra photographs of various members of her family and for making so many appearances in my own photographs!
Susie and Roger for their wonderful hospitality during the production process.
Vicky and Zophia for their photographs.
My photography friends, Vicky, Geoff, Simon and Steve, for their encouragement and support.
Joy and Joanne at Cotswold Keepsakes for their help and products.
The Scrapbook House and Eyelet Outlet for products.
Roz, Sophie and Juan at Search Press for their help and guidance and Roddy at Roddy Paine Photographic Studios for his excellent photographs of my work.

Cover
Pass the parcel

Page 1
William
Acetate overlays are a great way of adding meaning and depth to a scrapbook page. Eyelets provide the ideal means of attaching them. This acetate helps to enhance the theme of the page.

Opposite
Hong Kong years
I have printed my journaling on acetate here, painting underneath it to extend the idea of sand from the photograph appearing above the acetate.

Contents

Introduction

I started to create scrapbooks in 1997 following a visit to the States. I had always been a keen photographer and, with a large family, produced lots of photographs. Scrapbooking supplied a means of creating meaningful family albums and it was not long before my children were creating albums with me.

Once the basic cropping techniques have been mastered, scrapbookers usually want to start adding embellishments to their pages. The versatile eyelet kit then becomes an essential tool. Once you have started using eyelets, you will wonder how you ever scrapbooked without them!

In this book I aim to take you through the many uses of eyelets. I start with their essential attributes: for attaching vellum, acetate and fabric to your pages, without any risk of glue showing through and spoiling your project and with the added benefit of providing charming detail. I will then show you how you can use eyelets to add a range of other embellishments and accents including frames, mini-books, clasps, tags, charms and more. Eyelets come in a range of designs including letters, words and tiny replicas of items so that you can add detail and provide emphasis to your pages.

I hope you will be inspired by the ideas in the book so that you, too, believe that the eyelet tool kit was the best scrapbooking investment you ever made!

simple FUN

Winter

Winter

Sledging

On the evening of 27 January 2004, it snowed heavily. We woke the next morning to a winter wonderland and to announcements on the radio that school was closed. Martin couldn't get to work either. It was Kate's birthday so we got the sledges and dog and walked up through the woods into the valley picking up Maisie on the way. The children played for ages on the slopes in the meadow and Louise produced lots of warm drinks and flapjack. I think it was a perfect 13th birthday for Kate.

WifE

MUSICIAN

PHOTOGRAPHER

LOVER

MOTHER

SCRAPBOOKER

HOMEMAKER

Materials

Scrapbooking allows you to preserve your photographs and your memories. One of its great strengths is that everyone can develop their own scrapbooking style, linked to their interests in other crafts, such as painting, sewing, beading and stamping. The materials that can be used for scrapbooking are therefore almost infinite. However, as the craft is about preserving as well as displaying and recording, it is important that all materials which will touch your photographs are acid free, otherwise photographs can deteriorate, spoiling your scrapbooks. It is best to buy materials from reliable scrapbook sources and to check the labels to see that they are of archival quality, photo safe or acid free.

A guillotine large enough to cut scrapbooking cardstock.

Basic equipment

You do not actually need a lot to get started. The basics consist only of albums and paper or card and cutting, sticking and recording materials.

A cutting mat, mini guillotine, circle cutters, eraser, wavy ruler, pens and gel pens, coloured and graphite pencils, cork-backed metal ruler, photo-safe wax crayons, craft knife, embossing tool, scissors, PVA glue, glue pen, glue stick, photocare solution and pad, tweezers, photo tabs, double-sided tape, repositionable adhesive on a runner and glue dots.

A **guillotine** capable of cutting 30.5 x 30.5cm (12 x12in) card – the basic scrapbooking size – is helpful for cutting card and paper neatly and quickly. A smaller **trimmer** or **guillotine** is useful for smaller pieces of card and for photographs.

   Scissors are essential. I use a very small sharp pair for close cropping work.

   A craft knife allows you to cut very accurately, for example for hand-cut titles or where precise measurements are important such as for mosaics. It is used with a **cork-backed metal ruler** (to prevent slipping) and a **self-healing cutting mat**. My mat is slightly larger than a 30.5 x 30.5cm (12 x12in) scrapbook page and is ideal. It also has measurements marked on it which prove very useful. The cutting mat is also essential for use with the various **cutting tools** available, such as **circle** and **oval cutters**. A **wavy ruler** is fun for different cutting effects – see the last project in this book.

   Adhesives come in many guises and you will probably need a variety for different purposes. **Double-sided photo tabs** and **tape** are useful for adhering cardstock, paper and photographs. **Glue pens** and **water-based adhesive** are useful for attaching embellishments. Use **glue dots** for the heavier ones. Regular **PVA glue** or **glue stick** are good when making items from cardstock, such as covering frames. **Repositionable adhesive** (available in a runner) is invaluable for attaching items temporarily that you might want to move later, for example in mosaic and collage work.

Pens, **pencils** and **crayons** can help to make your pages really distinctive and are great for adding that personal touch. My favourites are fine-tipped marker pens. **Graphite pencils** are useful for measuring and drafting journaling or titles and can be rubbed out later with an ordinary **eraser**. I find **computer fonts** invaluable for journaling and titles too. I use them when I want a more 'published' look.

A **photo-safe wax crayon** is helpful for marking cutting lines on photographs which can be rubbed out later using a cloth. Finally, when I have completed a page, I always go over the photographs with a **photocare solution** and cloth before placing it in the album. This removes any fingerprints and sticky marks.

Albums, cardstock and paper

Albums need to be acid free. They come in a variety of sizes: 30.5 x 30.5cm (12 x12in) is the most popular, and all the projects in this book are for this size. Another standard size is 21.5 x 28cm (8.5 x11in), but this is not so popular in the UK. Smaller sizes: 20.3 x 20.3cm (8 x 8in) and 15.2 x 15.2cm (6 x 6in) are also available and are nice as gift albums.

The type of album I find the easiest to work with is called a **top-loading album**. All finished layouts are loaded into page protectors, which are then secured in an album, usually on metal posts. I find these **post-bound albums** the easiest. You can rearrange the finished pages in any order you like and add extra pages, so that you don't have to work chronologically. **Strap-bound albums** are also popular. With these you work straight on to the page but you can remove pages from the album to work on or to rearrange them. The pages are fixed to straps in the album.

Paper comes in varying thicknesses, colours and designs. The main thing is to ensure that it is acid and lignin free. Lignin causes the paper to go brown and crumble. The thicker 30.5 x 30.5cm (12 x 12in) paper is called **cardstock** and usually forms a sturdy background to any layout. Thinner paper and card is often used to provide added interest and enhance pages. There is a whole variety of designs and what each person chooses will be determined by the layout being created and individual taste. When using patterned paper, make sure it doesn't detract from your photographs, which you usually want to be the main focus of a page. There are also some lovely **speciality papers** available, such as **vellum** and **textured paper** or **mesh**, which can be used to create more individual effects. This book shows how to attach these using eyelets.

Acetate

I absolutely love this! Sheets of acetate come with pre-printed colour or plain black designs and are wonderful for adding depth to a page. They come in a variety of sizes and often include words, sayings or thoughts which can help you to convey a message or emotion on your layout. You can also print your own journaling on acetates. I think that eyelets are the best way of attaching acetate to the page.

Eyelet tool kit

This kit is used to fix eyelets to your scrapbook pages. The method is demonstrated on pages 12 and 13. It is possible to fix as many as six layers of paper, cardstock or photographs with the standard 3mm ($\frac{1}{8}$in) eyelet.

The **hole punch** makes holes in paper or cardstock. It is possible to attach different heads to make different sized holes, depending on the size of eyelet chosen for the particular project.

The **hammer** is used to hammer the hole punch through the work.

The **setter** is used with the hammer to 'set' the eyelet in the hole.

The **setting mat** is used with all eyelet work to avoid making holes in your work surface! It is not vital to have a separate mat. I use the back of my self-healing cutting mat which I find more convenient for larger pieces of work, preserving the front of the mat for when I need to cut or measure.

The **piercing tool** is essential for removing paper debris from the hole punch. It is also extremely useful for marking out measured holes before punching and for pre-making holes to attach other items, such as brads or beads.

Other types of eyelet tool kit

There are a number of other eyelet tool kits now on the market. They all work on the same principle, which is to make a hole in the papers and to set the eyelet. One I have tried uses a twisting motion and another a spring action, instead of hammering. The type chosen is a matter of individual choice. I find the one featured here simple and effective – especially for getting through a number of layers. It is noisy, however, because of the hammering.

Eyelets and charms

Eyelets are one of the most versatile embellishments for scrapbooks but also have a practical use: they are extremely sturdy and are ideal for fastening vellum, acetate and fabrics where glue might show through. They are wonderful for providing a means of hanging or threading fibres, ribbon and other embellishments.

They come in an almost endless variety of shapes and three basic sizes: 1mm (¹/₁₆in), 3mm (¹/₈in) and the larger, or shaped, eyelets in 4mm (³/₁₆in). I find the most useful size is the standard round 3mm (¹/₈in), in every colour of the rainbow! These are the ones I use most frequently. However, it is also possible to purchase eyelets with slightly longer or even very long stems. These are excellent if you want to fix a number of pieces of paper and card together, for example when making a tag or mini-book.

In addition to fixing together paper and related products, eyelets can also be used to attach charms. These range from letters to shapes, metal-rimmed tags, bookplates and a whole selection of metal hinges. Eyelets are ideal for attaching all of these firmly to layouts. Together with the charms, they add texture and dimension to layouts, which help to make them more interesting. The tiny 1mm (¹/₁₆in) eyelets can add charming detail to intricate embellishments but are fiddly to work with.

There is a whole range of eyelets in different shapes, from stars and flowers to animals and trinkets. In addition to having a practical function, these also help to add emphasis to layouts (see pages 36–41).

Eyelets can also be found with letters, words or phrases, which help to provide or add impact to journaling on a page.

Embellishments

These are the equivalent of the icing on the cake! The number of embellishments now available for scrapbook pages is enormous. It is tempting to use loads of them but I think they are best used sparingly to add a little finishing touch rather than to overwhelm the page. Some of the many available include:

Fibres, **thread**, **ribbons** and even **tinsel**! Great for hanging and threading charms, buttons, beads and tags. These are some of the most versatile embellishments for helping to add emphasis to the theme of a page. Depending on the choice, you can make your page feel rustic, using string or raffia, romantic, using pastel ribbons and highly decorated netting, seasonal, with tinsel or gold and silver threads, or masculine, with dark ginghams or leather thread.

Wires and chains Like fibre and ribbon, when used in conjunction with eyelets, these are useful for hanging things from and to add to the 'feel' of a page.

Fabric and **twill tape** have also become popular. It is possible to stamp and paint them and print on them using the computer.

Stickers, **feathers**, **beads**, **silk flowers**, **metal clasps** and **labels** can be used to add detail and emphasis.

Memorabilia Do not neglect your own tickets, tokens, cards, stamps, cigarette cards, leaflets, maps and other memorabilia. Not only do they add detail and dimension but they also make your pages truly personal. With the photographs, they are often the most interesting part of a scrapbook. It is best to spray memorabilia from an unknown source with archival mist before adhering them to your pages to ensure archival quality is preserved.

Slide mounts are very versatile as you can cover them in any paper to make them tone with your page. I prefer the card rather than plastic ones because you can punch holes in them (see page 20). They can be used to emphasise part of a photograph, highlight a word or frame another embellishment, or they can be made into individual shaker boxes.

A slide mount, ribbons, threads, tinsel, feathers, postage stamps, fabric and other stickers, cigarette cards, labels, a metal label, metal clasps, beads, silk flowers and a plug chain.

Other materials

Like embellishments, there is a huge variety of other materials available. What you use may depend largely upon what other crafts you enjoy.

Paint, acrylic and watercolour, **gesso** and **texture paste** can all create interesting additions to your pages. I frequently use them to paint backgrounds, using **brushes** and **foam rollers** in various designs for different effects. **Rub-on paints** are best applied with your finger and can be used for distressing, ageing or providing a rustic look on the layout.

Craft punches can be used to make a variety of shapes from paper, cardstock or photographs.

Rubber stamps, **foam stamps** and **inkpads** add detail to pages and can also be used for lettering. **Watermark stamp pads** can be used with stamps and chalks for a subtle background motif.

Chalks, **sandpaper** and **inks** are particularly useful to add age, texture and definition to a page.

Embossing powder and a **heating tool** can be used with an **embossing pen**, **pad** or stamps to add raised, textured detail to a page in a variety of finishes. You can create some stylish embellishments and the finished look has a wonderful texture and gloss. **Gold-** and **silver-leafing pens** can also be used for titles or the edges of cards. All of these are great for wedding or anniversary celebration pages and heritage.

Rub-on transfers, commonly in letter form, are great for creating words.

Adhesive remover is one of the most useful products around, and allows you to unstick anything without leaving marks should you change your mind.

I use a **protractor** to cut cardstock at precise angles, for example when making a triangular frame.

Letter or shape **stencils** are used for creating handwritten lettering or to make shapes from a particular paper or cardstock to coordinate with the layout.

Craft punches, foam and rubber stamps, walnut ink, embossing powder, rub-on transfers, a watermark stamp pad, sandpaper, dye inkpad, foam roller, protractor, rub-on paints, acrylic paints and paint brush, adhesive remover, stencil, heating tool, gold-leafing pen and stickers.

Techniques

One of the great advantages of using eyelets in your scrapbooks is the ease with which the technique of eyelet setting can be mastered. The technique remains the same whatever type of eyelet you choose for your scrapbook layout. I have used the tool kit demonstrated here for all the layouts in this book as I find it simple and effective, though the hammering makes it noisy. There are other types of kit available, as explained on page 8.

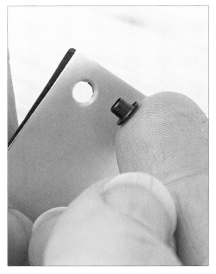

1. Always work on a setting mat or on the back of your cutting mat. This avoids making holes in your work surface or the measuring side of your cutting mat. Place the eyelet piercing tool where you want to put the eyelet in your layered card or paper. Tap the tool with the hammer reasonably hard. As a rough rule of thumb I usually say one tap of the hammer for each layer of paper you are trying to go through.

2. Place the eyelet through the hole.

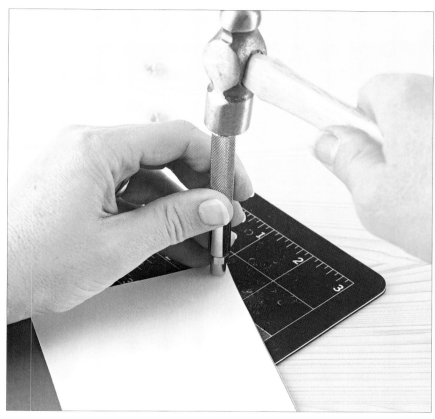

3. Place the end of the setting tool in the back of the eyelet and tap it with the hammer. I usually tap the tool two or three times to set an eyelet.

4. The setting tool presses open the back of the eyelet and fixes it in place.

The secured eyelet shown from the front.

Tip

The hole punch does have a tendency to become clogged with card and paper. I find the easiest way to clean it is to use the piercing tool to empty it.

13

Attaching vellum

Vellum is a semi-transparent paper that is wonderful for adding dimension to scrapbook pages. It allows what is underneath to show through and sometimes provides a subtle or softening change of colour. It comes either plain (as in the 'Austria' example opposite) or coloured. Sometimes it is patterned as well – as in the other examples on these pages. Although vellum looks wonderful on layouts it can be really troublesome to fix because virtually every glue-based fixing product shows through, which spoils the effect. Eyelets are the answer! They not only solve this problem but also add dimension and detail of their own.

Sarah – bridesmaid

Given that this is a photograph of me (longer ago than I care to remember), I hesitate to call it 'heritage' style! However, that is the look I have gone for. The vellum incorporates a heritage-style design and I have enhanced the soft feel of the page by measuring out an inner frame, cutting it out with a craft knife and then tearing the inner edges. Heart-shaped eyelets complete the romantic feel.

Venice

Printed vellum has been used for the title on this page. I printed it on the computer and embossed it whilst the printing ink was still wet. Fixing the vellum over the photograph helps to give an impression of the place. The eyelets were chosen to complement the theme. Note that it is important to emboss the vellum before fixing it to the photograph, otherwise you might melt the photograph.

Austria

I drew and cut round a dinner plate to make the circle in the plain vellum and embossed the inner edge. Four eyelets fix the vellum to the page. The vellum map and crest were printed from the internet.

Dogs are just children with fur

A little bit of snow sends my dog into skittish mood! I have emphasised the snow in the photographs with the white spotted vellum. This has been fixed with red eyelets. Placing the title under the vellum and the embossed snowflake embellishment over it helps to add depth to the page.

Attaching acetate

Like vellum, acetate is a wonderfully versatile medium which allows you to add depth to a scrapbook page. Since it is completely transparent, anything placed underneath it will be more visible than when using vellum. Acetate comes pre-printed in a variety of sizes and designs. When words form part of the acetate's design, they can really help to emphasise the theme of the layout. Alternatively, you can use plain acetate and print your own journaling or titles using a computer.

Tip

Acetates are made in two types: smooth on both sides for laser printers or with one rough side for ink-jet printers. I have an ink-jet printer and print on the rough reverse of the acetate. This avoids changing the print set-up on the computer and the ink dries immediately. Behind a page protector, the fact that you have printed on the rough side of the acetate is not visible.

For the 'Snow Day' layout, I printed the text on an A4 sheet of acetate using a number of different fonts. I cut a piece of watercolour paper to the same size and made pencil marks to indicate where the bands of colour should go, behind the lettering. I then painted the paper in my choice of colours, allowing the paint to dry before attaching the paper and then the acetate to the layout.

Snow day

When snow falls in the village where I live, it looks really beautiful. I had this photograph enlarged to 45.7 x 30.5cm (18 x 12in) and cut it to fit across two pages. The words printed on the acetate remind me of one of the lovely 'Snow Days' in 2004.

Emma

A 30.5 x 30.5cm (12x12in) acetate has been cut up to provide emphasis on two sides of the photograph, with paint and stamped motifs underneath adding to the theme. If the acetate contains a lot of wording it can overwhelm the photograph if placed on top. In these circumstances, the acetate can be more effective cropped, as here.

Play

By contrast, the whole acetate could be used here, as the wording is unobtrusive. Note that the blue printing picks out the colour of Annie's jacket, helping to make the layout coherent.

Attaching fabric

It is increasingly popular to use fabric and ribbon on scrapbook pages. They add texture and interest. However, as with vellum and acetate, attaching them with glue can prove hazardous because it shows through, particularly with mesh, gauze and fine ribbon. Eyelets are an ideal alternative and go through fabric easily.

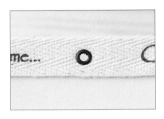

1. Apply repositionable adhesive to the back of the twill tape.

2. Stick the tape on to the card to keep it taut. Then make a hole in it using the hammer and hole punching tool on a setting mat or the back of your cutting mat.

3. Do not worry if you cannot see a neat circular hole, as when piercing card or paper. The hole in the tape will hardly show, but it will be there nonetheless.

4. Push the eyelet in and set it in the usual way.

Once upon a time

A layout featuring all the family reading one relaxing summer holiday. The twill tape forms a binding and the layout opens out like a book. It can either be slipped into a page protector in its entirety and taken out to look at, or stuck with photo tabs on the outside of the page protector so that it is possible to open it out each time someone looks at the album.

Autumn

This is one of my favourite layouts in the book, evoking a misty, late autumn afternoon in the woods near my home. I replicated the soft feel of the photograph by subtle use of coloured ink sprayed on to the background card from a spray bottle. Sheer ribbon and mesh in autumn colours, attached with eyelets, enhance the theme. Note that it would not have been possible to use any form of glue on the ribbon or mesh without it showing through and spoiling the layout.

Hunt the washing pole

Ribbon has been attached to labels and journaling with enclosed eyelets (called snaps), and then the ribbon has been used to hang the labels from pegs on string, like a washing line.

Hanging & threading

If there is one thing that the eyelet was designed for, it is for hanging or threading and there is a whole range of materials that can be used for this purpose, from chains and wire to ribbon, string, twine and thread.

The technique shown below can be used to cover any size of card frame as well as slide mounts.

1. Apply glue stick to the back of the slide mount and stick it to the paper. Use a craft knife to cut across the corners as shown and then cut a cross in the middle of the aperture.

2. Glue the front of the slide mount and snip off the points from the two triangular flaps that will cover the sides of the mount.

3. Fold back the edges of the paper and stick them down as shown.

4. Set an eyelet in the covered slide mount in the usual way and thread a length of plug chain through it.

Tip

The loose end of the chain slots into the fastener. This can be quite fiddly. The smaller the chain, the fiddlier it is. Make sure you use a chain that is small enough to fit through the eyelet.

It's the shades!

I have used the slide mounts and chains, patterned paper and embellishments to emphasise the theme of the page – the amazing psychedelic pink sunglasses that my children took to wearing for a couple of summers!

Stockings

The stocking opening ceremony is a big tradition in our family and with six of us it can take as long as two hours! I have made my own stocking tags using stickers and eyelets, and I have embossed the edges and hung them from festive gold fibre.

Adventure

Here I have threaded wire through eyelets and made journaling, photographs and titles into impromptu tags.

Lucy

Eyelets have been used for hanging both titles here but in different ways, one vertically and one horizontally.

On the farm

I have added a rustic feel to this layout by my choice of materials and techniques, including undyed string, ink and cork, and tearing and chalking photographs. The stamped background was made using a garden fern leaf dipped in acrylic paint and stamped on to the page.

Frames & borders

Eyelets are perfect for providing an eye-catching method of making frames and borders. They can be used with thread, string, ribbon, flax and fibres to highlight pages, journaling or individual photographs in a variety of ways.

2. Pierce holes and attach and set the eyelets in the usual way. Take your chosen thread and stick down the end on the back of the piece, then begin threading through the eyelets.

1. Draw a pencil line and mark the position of the eyelet holes with a piercing tool. Use an eraser to rub out the pencil line.

3. Continue threading the border in a shoelace pattern.

Sledging

This was a wonderful and unexpected day off school in 2004. We walked up through the woods to visit friends in the next valley and the children spent hours sledging. I have emphasised the fun and action by arranging the photographs at irregular angles and by adding the eyelet and fibre border. The red and yellow fibre coordinates with the colours in the photographs.

On the evening of 27 January 2004, it snowed heavily. We woke the next morning to a winter wonderland and to announcements on the radio that school was closed. Martin couldn't get to work either. It was Kate's birthday so we got the sledges and dog and walked up through the woods into her valley, picking up Maisie on the way. The children played for ages on the sledges in the meadow and Louise produced lots of warm drinks and flapjack. I think it was a perfect 13th birthday for Kate.

Simple fun

This is one of my favourite action shots. Nicholas spent a happy summer's afternoon bouncing on his trampoline for me and as his stance became more open, so did his smile! I did not want to over-complicate the page, as the photograph speaks for itself, so I have kept the design simple, like the title.

Giggle

For me, the photograph said it all. I wanted to keep it simple so the ribbon and eyelet border with its triangular cardstock corners just draws the eye into the photograph.

Charlie

This layout shows the subtle use of snaps. The four corners of the cardstock have been folded very lightly, so as not to crease the edge completely flat, and fixed with snaps in the corner. This is one of my favourite ways of framing a page or photograph, because it helps draw the eye into the layout. For this technique cardstock with different colours or patterns on each side works particularly well.

Emma – bridesmaid

In contrast to the 'Giggle' example on page 25, the eyelets here are placed just outside the photograph but still on the contrasting red cardstock mat. The gold string forms a very subtle frame and the eyelets along the green strip at the top of the layout provide a contrasting border.

Rest and relaxation

This is one of my favourite frames using eyelets. The four eyelets have been set into the actual photograph and string is threaded through the holes and knotted on the front of the layout, emphasising the focal point of the photograph. I have also added a tiny tag through one eyelet and an eyelet word.

Moreton Show

I created the central montage working from the outside edge inwards, overlaying some of the elements. I measured and spaced the eyelets for this border using the technique shown on page 24 and then threaded raffia through the eyelet holes for a rustic feel. I finished by using brown rub-on paint around the outer edge of the cardstock.

Impressions of Norway

Here I have created a border made entirely of ribbon, which has been threaded through four holes, one in each corner of the page, and fixed to the back of the layout using the technique shown on page 24. The outsized snowflake eyelets have been fixed into the same holes, helping to secure the ribbon.

Mini-books

Mini-books have many uses. They are great for including a number of photographs where you have a lot from one event but do not want to create lots of individual layouts. They make perfect gifts – especially for birthdays or occasions such as Mother's Day. They are useful for including extra journaling – particularly if you have things to say that you would rather keep hidden from the casual viewer of your album!

This demonstration shows how to make a mini-book based on a cross design.

1. Mark out the cardstock into nine equal squares, each of sides 7.5cm (3in).

2. Cut out the corner squares.

3. Rub out the lines and fold in the sides.

4. Stick on the photographs and add any embellishments.

5. Measure, mark and make eyelet holes in the layout, using the folded mini-book as a guide. Set the eyelets and thread string through them using the technique shown on page 24. Fix the centre of the mini-book to the background cardstock using photo tabs, then knot the string.

Travellers' fair

I took lots of photographs at the fair, which I wanted to include in the album to give a full flavour of the event but without showcasing all of them. I therefore included them in a mini-book.

Christmas mini-book

This is a variation on the Travellers' fair book. The two sidepieces have been cut into measured points, eyelets set and ribbon threaded through. Green cardstock has been journaled, cut to size and stuck over the sides and base of the book. When tied up (left), the mini-book gives the impression of a parcel – great for Christmas, birthdays or celebrations!

Mini-books and page protectors

If you use the type of album where pages slip in to page protectors (called top-loading), then opening the mini-book to look at it can be a problem. There are two solutions. One is to slip the whole page, including the mini-book, into the page protector. The viewer then needs to extract the whole page to look at the mini-book. The alternative, and the example shown here, is to make a hole in the page protector to attach the book or clasp, sticking the mini-book on the outside of the page protector. That way, the rest of the page remains protected.

The Louvre

The mini-book has been made from pieces of cardstock, which have been folded concertina style. Note that the book can be made as large as you wish by sticking facing pieces of cardstock together. The photographs were cut to size and fixed on both sides of the book. The eyelet clasp was fitted last. The ribbon was fixed to the underside of the backing cardstock with sticky tape and then pulled through the page protector as shown below.

1. I marked the place for the hole on top of the page protector with photo-safe wax crayon. I then slid the setting mat between the layout and the page protector, made the hole using the hole punch and hammer, then removed the mat.

2. The ribbon was attached to the back of the layout and threaded through the eyelet hole. I then placed the layout in the page protector and fastened the mini-book to the outside of the page protector with photo tabs. Next I put one hand inside the page protector to guide the ribbon through the hole before fastening it to the clasp on the outside of the mini-book in the usual way.

Paris

This mini-book (based on an idea by Joy Aitman) was made using one piece of 30.5 x 30.5cm (12x12in) cardstock, cut into two pieces, one measuring 16.5cm (6½in) and the other 14cm (5½in). The larger piece was folded in half before sticking the smaller piece to it horizontally. I then stuck the photographs into the book, adding embellishments. The technique shown opposite was used to stick the mini-book to the outside of the page protector.

Home

Pages have been cut to accommodate the photograph on the front cover of the mini-book, i.e. 16.5 x 11.5cm (6½ x 4½in). The mini-book was assembled using a collage style. Eyelets were set on the front cover of the book only, and holes were made in identical places on remaining pages. String was threaded through the holes and eyelets and tied to assemble the finished mini-book.

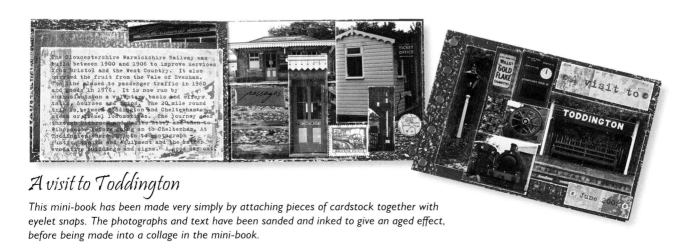

A visit to Toddington

This mini-book has been made very simply by attaching pieces of cardstock together with eyelet snaps. The photographs and text have been sanded and inked to give an aged effect, before being made into a collage in the mini-book.

Tags

Tags are useful for adding accents or dimension to a scrapbook page. Tags can be purchased ready made or you can make your own in any style, colour and design that you wish! Eyelets and tags were meant for each other. Eyelets can be used to fix the tags to the page, provide a means of threading or hanging or just to add that finishing touch.

Family matters

Here I have printed the family names as labels. The tags form simple titles.

Brothers

This page is a personal favourite. It shows an old photograph of my father and his eldest brother, now sadly dead. They were very close. I bought these tags, fixed on the letter stickers and stuck the tags to the page as a title, using rub-on paints to coordinate colour with the page.

Seasons

If you are using tags for a title, you do not have to restrict yourself to one letter per tag. Here the tags, made from paper depicting the different months of the year, form a background to the titles of the four seasons.

Tag books

Eyelets can be bought with longer stems which are useful for chunkier items or for making tag books. In these examples, the eyelets in the 'Wild thing' frame and in the 'Winter' tag book are longer than normal, and the eyelet fixing the 'Farm' tag is extra-long. A stock of different sizes proves invaluable. Eyelet tags, like mini-books, make attractive presents as well as items for scrapbook pages.

Seville

Eyelet hinges have been used as part of this tag.

Wild thing

I made a cardstock frame to fit the focal point of the photograph and covered it using the technique shown on page 20.

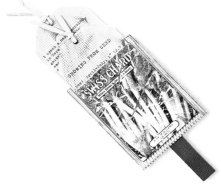

The vegetable patch

I made a pocket using a seed packet, which I distressed by crumpling it and then using sandpaper and ink. The tags were slipped in the pocket.

Farm

This is one of my favourites, using lots of photographs and rustic embellishments. A long-stemmed eyelet was used to fix the book together and additional eyelets were used with the word 'spring' on one of the tags.

Winter

I made three tags the same size. I put journaling on one, stamped and embossed a tree on another and fixed a photograph on the third, making a little tag book.

Eyelets as accents

Eyelets in all their various guises can be used to make accents with other embellishments, or as tiny accents in their own right. This is where they are at their most versatile and the only limit is your imagination!

Tiny 1mm ($^1/_{16}$in) eyelets have been used as car wheels.

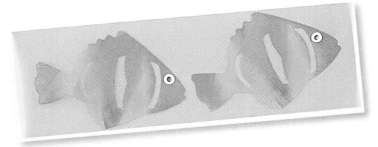

3mm ($^1/_8$in) white eyelets make eyes for these stamped fish and also fix the vellum to the card.

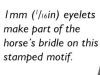 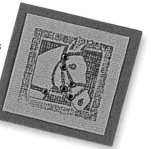

1mm ($^1/_{16}$in) eyelets make part of the horse's bridle on this stamped motif.

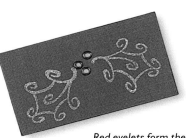

Red eyelets form the berries for the stamped holly leaves.

White eyelets are used to fix the acetate to this summer scene made from cardstock, paper, a stamped umbrella and a punched sun.

This Christmas slide mount has been decorated with seasonal eyelets.

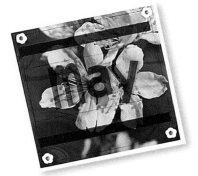

The May acetate is complemented with flower-shaped eyelets to match the photograph beneath.

This banner has been accented with little musical note-shaped eyelets.

Lilo

This is one of my favourite layouts. Total relaxation! I have applied acrylic paint to the background cardstock with a textured roller. The seahorse, which helps to highlight the theme of the page, is made from white and turquoise acrylic paint mixed together and stamped on with a stamp from a hardware store. Eyelets have been used to make the seahorse's eye and spine.

Trimming the tree

This is an annual tradition in our family. The girls now have it off to a fine art! The tree accents have been made using paper, cardstock and parts of photographs. The eyelets echo the decorations on the tree. They have also been used to trap the tinsel behind the title printed on vellum, which again emphasises the subject matter of the layout.

Aspects of Me

I have chosen this project for three reasons. First, many scrapbookers forget to put themselves in their albums at all. This is to encourage you to do so! Future generations will want to know about you as well as the rest of your friends and family, otherwise there will be an important part of the jigsaw missing.

Secondly, it is one of the only decent photographs I have ever seen of me! Most of the time I am the other side of the lens. I had the photograph taken professionally and strongly recommend that you treat yourself. It really wasn't that scary!

Thirdly, the page can be adapted to any other person you want to showcase in your album, or even a group shot. Eyelets, papers and embellishments were used to complement the words on the 'crossword'. You need to choose styles to complement your own descriptions. My photograph was 14.2 x 18.8cm ($5^5/_8$ x $7^3/_8$in). If you have a standard 12.7 x 17.8cm (5 x 7in) sized photograph, you could mat it to fit these dimensions.

You will need

Turquoise cardstock, 30.5 x 30.5cm (12 x 12in)

A photograph of you

Photo tabs

Printed papers to suit your descriptions: I have used check floor, music, greetings, word definition, clocks and handwritten style papers

Scrap paper and pen

Metal letters with eyelet holes

Letter stickers: I have used black stencil, red, silver, circle-framed, variable font and numbered

Ribbons: I have used gingham and lace

Eyelets: I have used plain red, musical note, word, yellow and red heart

Craft knife and cutting mat

Eyelet tool kit

Brads: I have used a flower and a star

Embellishments: I have used a metal heart and a strip of old film negative

Ruler

1. Stick the photograph on the cardstock using photo tabs.

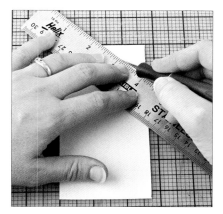

2. To make a tag, take a rectangle of printed paper. Measure and mark 2.5cm (1in) down from the top, and mark this point on the sides. Mark the midpoint of the top edge. Draw a line from the midpoint to the mark on the side, and cut off the corner. Repeat the other side to make the tag shape.

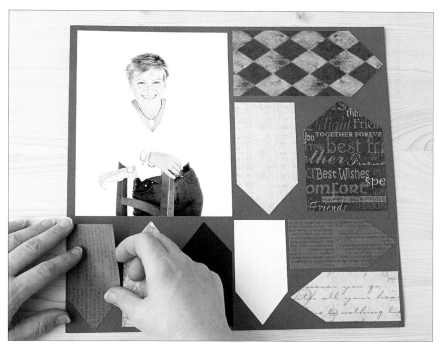

3. Cut rectangles and make tag shapes from all the various types of paper and attach them as shown using photo tabs. Your tags should fit the spaces left by your photograph. My rectangles were, top: 14.5 x 7.2cm (5¾ x 2⅞in); middle left: 11.5 x 5.8cm (4½ x 2¼in); middle right: 11.5 x 7.5cm (4½ x 3in); bottom row all 9.6 x 4.8cm (3¾ x 1⅞in).

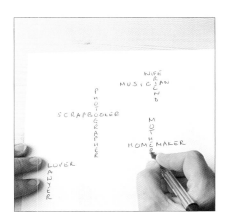

4. I chose nine words to describe me as there are nine tags. Practise writing your chosen words crossword style as shown. When arranging them on the page, I made sure that each tag had part of a word on it.

5. I have used metal letters to spell out the word 'wife'. To fix metal letters, first place them on the layout in the desired arrangement. Then mark where the eyelet will go by using a paper piercing tool. Next attach each letter individually with eyelets.

The finished project. Add the remaining lettering using your handwritten design as a guide. Apart from the word 'wife', I have used stickers for all the lettering. I have chosen black, red and sand-coloured stickers in various different designs. Next, I have fixed eyelets, brads or ribbon to the point of each tag, complementing the words with the style of eyelet where possible. Finally I have added a couple of other embellishments such as the old film negative stuck on with glue and the metal heart.

31ST OCTOBER 2004

POSITIVELY DEFRIGHTFUL!

The children had planned their costumes for weeks! They went out trick-or-treating. — Apparently this custom originated with beggars wandering from village to village and promising to say prayers on behalf of the dead relatives of donors of the "treat" (NICE!!) In those days, the "treat" was currant bread, not sweets. In reality the customs of Halloween grew out of the rituals of the Celts celebrating a new year and out of the medieval prayer rituals of Europeans.

Halloween

The Halloween-style eyelets are both functional and decorative. They have been used to attach the vellum to the cardstock but also as accents in themselves. I have cut round the figures in the photographs to accentuate the subject and dispose of distracting backgrounds. The titles were printed on vellum with embossing powder added to part of the writing just after printing, before the ink dried. The embossing powder was then heated to a raised shine using a heating tool.

Spring in Marlow

Flower eyelets have been used as part of the letters and to affix the journaling, helping to emphasise the spring theme.

Wet

I have used eyelets as part of the letters to accentuate the title and the impression of water.

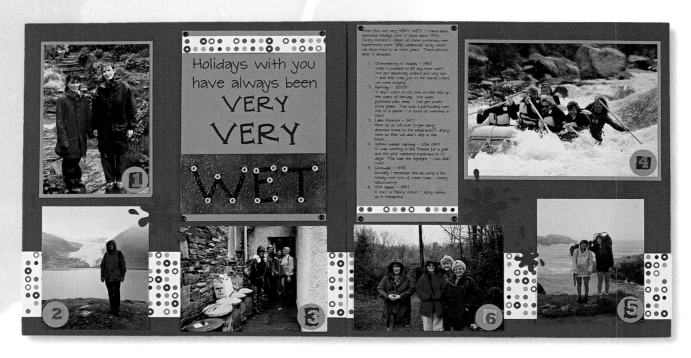

Skiing

I have used lots of different snow- and holiday-related eyelets as accents, including various eyelet words, so that a collage effect is created from eyelets and other embellishments. The edge of the background cardstock was embossed using part of a snowflake stamp and white embossing powder, heated with a heating tool.

Messing About on the River

The idea with this project is to cut photographs and card in wavy lines to emphasise the water theme. The eyelets are placed to add a sense of movement and to give an impression of water droplets. This project could be adapted to any water-based photographs such as seaside, lakes, swimming pool, water sports or even a child playing with a sprinkler in the garden!

You will need

Two pieces of dark blue cardstock, 30.5 x 30.5cm (12 x 12in)

Three pieces of pale blue cardstock in the same size

Cream cardstock in the same size

Wavy ruler

Pencil and eraser

Photo tabs

Photographs

Photo-safe wax crayon

Circle cutter and cutting mat

Twelve plain white eyelets

Eyelet tool kit

Brown ship's wheel card embellishment and glue pen

'We Are Family' button embellishment and glue dot

Scissors

1. Use the wavy ruler to draw a line on the blue cardstock.

2. Cut out the shape and mount it on the pale blue cardstock using photo tabs.

3. Draw on the photograph using photo-safe wax crayon and a wavy ruler to match the dark blue wavy line on the cardstock.

4. Stick the photograph on to a second piece of pale blue cardstock using photo tabs.

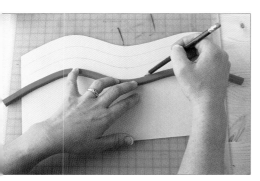

5. Draw three wavy bands on the cream card.

6. Mount the cream wavy line on the left-hand scrapbook page. Use a circle cutter to cut out the chosen part of one photograph.

Tip
The wavy line does not need to follow the wave of the cardstock strip exactly. If they are slightly different, this adds to the impression of movement.

7. Use the circle cutter to make a dark blue mat for this photograph. Mount one wavy cream band on the left-hand page, with the matted circular photograph on top. Draw a wavy pencil line on the cream band using the wavy ruler and pierce holes where the eyelets will be fixed. Rub out the pencil line.

The finished project. I printed my title and journaling on pale blue cardstock before mounting them on the dark blue cardstock. All photographs and mats were adhered using photo tabs. I used a glue dot for the button as these are very good for heavier embellishments and a glue pen for the ship's wheel as the pen provided a neat, thin line of glue.

8. Set eyelets where pierced holes have been made. Assemble the wavy bands, photographs and journaling for both pages as shown. Then add the final embellishments.

Tip

Ensure that you rub out the pencil lines before setting the eyelets but after piercing. It is difficult to rub out pencil lines once the eyelets have been set.

Pass the parcel

The idea with all the layouts on these two pages and the 'Messing About on the River' project, is to use eyelets for emphasis. Here, I have used a dinner plate to draw the circle where the eyelets appear. Otherwise I have used the same techniques for arranging and setting the eyelets as in the project. I like the way the circle of eyelets and parcel stickers help to emphasise the subject of the layout.

Easter egg hunt

I have cut out little oval egg shapes, stamped them with gold ink and set eyelets in each of them before adding stickers to make the title. They have then been strung onto fibre. The title complements the photographs.

46